SIMPLE BEGINNINGS:
Beading

SIMPLE BEGINNINGS:
Beading

A Step-by-Step Guide for Creating Your Own Custom Jewelry

Suzann Sladcik Wilson

Design Originals

Blue Birds in Flight,
page 68.

Dedication:

This book is dedicated to my Father, William K. Sladcik. Thank you
for giving me the gift of creativity and for helping my dreams
come true. I love you!

Thank you to the following independent local bead stores for their help with this book:

Alya's Originals, Illinois (www.aylasoriginals.com, 877-328-2952)
The Bead Bucket/The Mother Bead, Wisconsin (www.themotherbead.com, 920-854-7047
or 920-437-2821),
Bodacious Beads, Illinois (www.BodaciousBeadschicago.com, 847-699-7959),
and Izora's Beads, Findings and Inspiration, Wisconsin (izorasbeads.com, 920-868-4222).

Photography by Suzann Sladcik and William K. Sladcik.

Special thanks to Euro Tool, Inc. for the use of the photos appearing on pages 13, 16, and 17.

ISBN 978-1-57421-415-4

Library of Congress Cataloging-in-Publication Data

Wilson, Suzann Sladcik.
 Simple beginnings : beading / Suzann Sladcik Wilson.
    p. cm.
 Includes index.
 ISBN 978-1-57421-415-4 (pbk.)
 1. Jewelry making. 2. Beadwork. I. Title.
 TT212.W56 2012
 739.27--dc23
              2011032431

About the Author

Author Suzann Sladcik Wilson. Photo by Alysa Correll Clark of Water Street Dreams.

Joy is the theme that runs through all of Suzann Sladcik Wilson's work. Whether she is designing an original piece of jewelry for a client, introducing a student to the joy of beading and jewelry design, or hosting or appearing as a guest on radio shows, her message is about empowerment through creativity and inspiration.

For more than eighteen years, Wilson has been and continues to be a master in her field. Using only the highest quality materials of Swarovski crystals, Hill Tribe silver, artisan beads, and more, Wilson creates beauty and joy in the form of earrings, necklaces, bracelets, and watches, and instructs her followers to do the same. In a time when many individuals are searching for something more, Wilson teaches all of her students how to maximize their minds, bodies, and spirits by using the power of jewelry design, coupled with the drive of their passions, to create and inspire.

As an artist, author, educator, consultant, entrepreneur, and philanthropist, Wilson is as successful as she is busy. Her blogs, articles, and jewelry designs have appeared all over the web and in print. In her professional jewelry design career, Wilson has been published in *Bead Style, Simply Beads Magazine, Bead Trends,* on the website *epatterns.com,* and in the books *Four Seasons of Beading* and *Earrings, Earrings, Earrings!.*

Wilson has been a guest on *Military Mom Radio* and *Motherhood Talk Radio,* each show reaching 60,000 listeners. Additionally, Wilson has been a substitute host on the Her Insight Radio Network. She is also a Professional Designer Member of the Craft and Hobby Association, and in January 2011 received the coveted Craft and Hobby Association Designer Press Kit award for an innovative necklace design. An active contributor and participant in many charities, Wilson strives to make the world a better place for today's and our future's children.

Suzann Sladcik Wilson was born in Chicago, Illinois. She attended Loyola University of Chicago, earning her Bachelor's Degree in Education. She continues to expand her professional knowledge of beading and jewelry making by attending the yearly Bead and Button Show in Milwaukee, Wisconsin, subscribing and contributing to several leading beading and jewelry-making magazines, and networking with several other leading designers.

Wilson currently splits her time between Chicago, Illinois, Door County, Wisconsin, and occasionally Frankfurt, Germany. You can learn more by visiting Suzann online at *Beadphoria.com, BeadphoriaBlog.com* or *www.BeadphoriaBoutique.com.*

Contents

Discover all you need to know about beading!

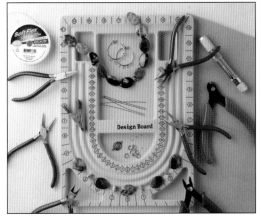

10 Tools of the trade.

18 Different kinds of beads.

32 Stringing materials.

34 Findings.

46 Step-by-step tutorials.

52 Creative projects.

82 Inspirational ideas.

Introduction:
Release Your Inner Jewelry Designer!

Remember the days when you were little and had a brand new box of crayons? All of those wonderful colors! You threw caution to the wind and started blending the colors together. When you were done, you had created a colorful work of art that brought a smile to your face. You can have that same exciting and creative experience making beaded jewelry.

Fight the urge to say, "I can't make jewelry! I'm not creative!" I have been teaching novice beaders for many years, and whenever I start a new class, at least one student doesn't believe he or she can create jewelry. I am here to silence that inner critic and bring out your inner jewelry designer.

Usually those who say they are not creative are the ones who actually end up with a life-long passion for beading. Why? Because they have learned the secret that so many talented jewelry makers know: Beading allows you to make a wearable work of art in a short amount of time using the colors, materials, and textures you love.

Beads call for you to experiment and play with color combinations in brand new ways, and there is no wrong way to design a piece—only your way. With beading, you are able to express your personal style and passion through jewelry. As you read this book, I will be with you every step of the way, with easy-to-follow instructions, practical hints and tips, and lots of encouragement to be the best you can be as you begin your fabulous journey into jewelry creation.

—Suzann Sladcik Wilson

Bountiful Harvest, page 62.

Tools

Many
of the tools a beader
uses can be found in the toolbox
sitting in a dark corner of the garage or
basement. While it might be temping to use these
readily available tools when first starting out, it is best
to purchase a set of tools specifically designed for jewelry
making. There are several reasons for this. First,
jewelry-making tools are specifically made to fit more
ergonomically in your hand, enabling you to easily perform
some of the intricate tasks required when making beaded
jewelry, and saving your hands from fatigue. This means you can
spend more time making your beautiful beaded creations.
Secondly, the jaws of standard pliers have ridges, while those
designed for jewelry making do not. Jewelry pliers will not
scratch the metal used to make your necklaces,
earrings, and bracelets. If you invest in a good set
of tools for your new passion, they will repay
you with years of fun creating your
wearable works of art.

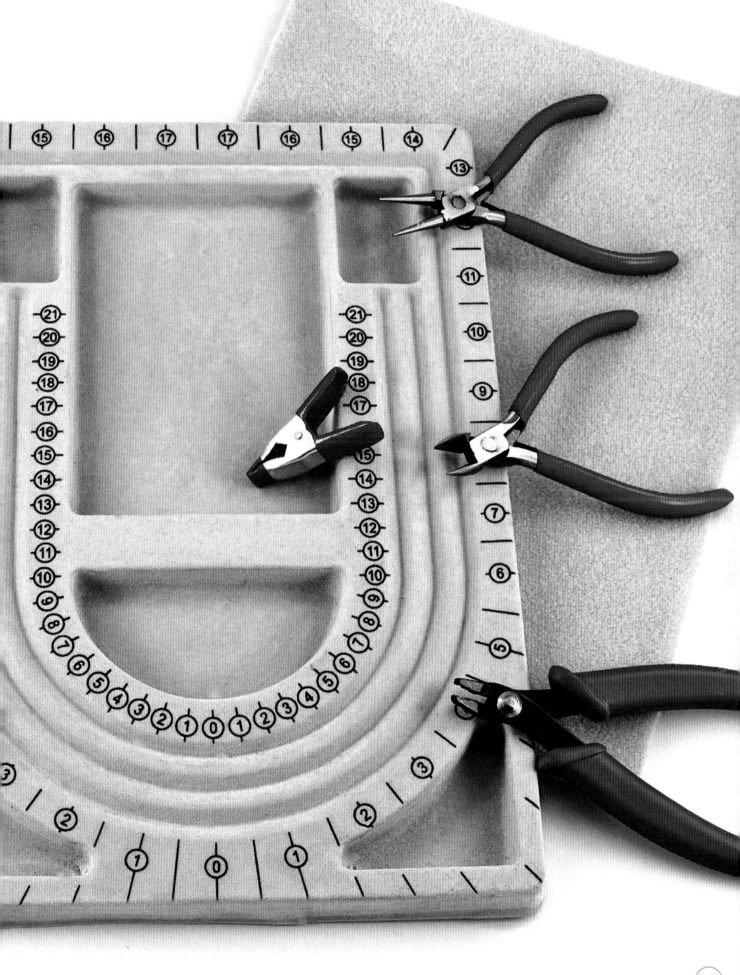

Toolbox Essentials

Bent-nose pliers

Certain tools are "must haves" if you are starting your journey into making beaded jewelry. After years of leading beginners into the world of jewelry design, these are the tools I have found to be absolute essentials. By building your tool kit with these fundamentals, you will have everything you need to make elegant earrings, beautiful bracelets, and knockout necklaces.

Pliers

Every beader should work with a reliable set of pliers. Pliers allow you to bend wire, make loops, get into hard-to-reach places, and add crimp tubes to a jewelry design. You can often find pliers designed specifically for beading as a set.

Chain-nose pliers

Bent-nose pliers: The jaws of bent-nose pliers are easy to identify, because they are tapered like regular "toolbox" pliers, but are then bent at an angle near the tip. These are the pliers to turn to when you need to get into tight spaces.

Chain-nose pliers: Chain-nose pliers, also known as needle-nose pliers, have a smooth flat surface on the interior of the jaws. The small tapered point allows you to get into small areas. You will typically use this tool for gripping jewelry findings and working with wire.

Crimping pliers

Crimping pliers: Crimping pliers are one of the cornerstone tools of beading and were designed specifically for jewelry making. Their purpose is to flatten and bend a small tube of metal, called a crimp tube or crimp, to securely finish a necklace or bracelet so your jewelry will stay together for years to come. When purchasing crimping pliers, make sure you buy regular-sized ones, not micro or mighty crimping pliers. Regular crimping pliers are meant for 2 x 2mm crimp tubes, which are what you will use when making most of your jewelry.

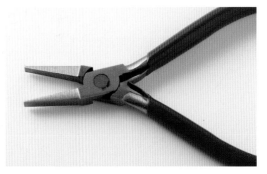
Flat-nose pliers

Flat-nose pliers: With large flat rectangular jaws, flat-nose pliers are useful for holding and bending wire. Flat-nose pliers give you the ability to grip objects tightly, because of their large surface area.

Round-nose pliers: The jaws of round-nose pliers are, of course, round, and taper to a point at each tip. The cone-like shape of each jaw enables you to make different-sized loops for earrings, pendants, and wirework. Round-nose pliers can also be utilized to help grip small areas.

Round-nose pliers

Other essentials

Don't forget these next few tools. They're also necessary items you will need in your toolbox.

Bead board: A bead board is to a jewelry maker what canvas is to a painter. Bead boards give you a place to lay your radiant beads out before stringing, so you can have a preview of your finished piece. There are many types of bead boards available. Most are gray and have one or more shallow channels. The best boards for beginners are flocked (covered in minute fiber particles) so your beads have a non-slip surface. I suggest beginning beaders purchase a necklace bead board with three channels, rather than just one. Not long after you start making jewelry, you will want to try making multi-strand necklaces, and with a three-channel board, you are equipped to do so. A bead board's outer channel is measured in inches, while the innermost channel is measured in centimeters.

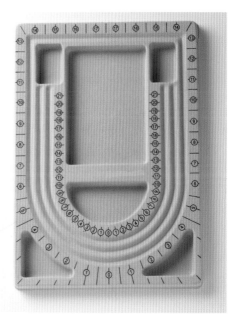

Bead board

Bead mat: These practical mats are soft, fuzzy, and will save you lots of frustration. Their wooly material keeps beads from rolling away from your jewelry-making area. Bead mats often come in many different colors. They are very inexpensive, so it is worth having a few on hand.

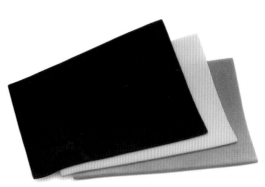

Bead mat. Photo supplied by Euro Tool, Inc.

Suzann's Sensational Beading Tip

If you find a place on the jaws of your round-nose pliers that makes a perfect-sized loop, take a permanent marker and mark the spot. By consistently using the same place on your pliers, you will always make loops of the same size.

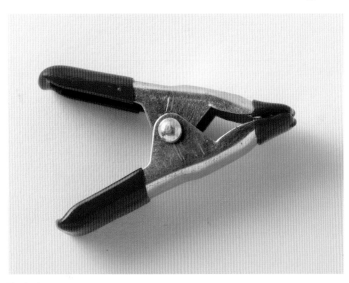

End clamp

End clamps: There is nothing more heartbreaking than picking up your beautiful necklace design after you have strung your all your beads and watching them fall off the other end. Over the years, I have tried many different methods of keeping my designs intact when moving them. The best solution I've discovered is the end clamp. End clamps are about 2" (51mm) long and have rubber tips. The rubber keeps the clamp in place without kinking your wire. Most beaders I know keep several in their toolbox to use on pieces in progress.

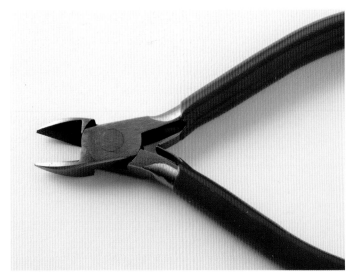

Wire cutters

Wire cutters: Wire cutters are the workhorse of your toolbox. You will use your wire cutters on everything from beading wire to head pins and eye pins. I recommend using flush cutters to obtain the straightest cuts. If your wire cutters are leaving burrs (jagged edges) or you need to use excessive force to complete a cut, the blades might be worn down and you may want to replace your cutters.

Toolbox Extras

After building the base of your tool kit, you might want to add on a few extras. These tools, although not essential for making strung jewelry, can make life much easier for jewelry makers. If your jewelry making turns into a passionate hobby or a career, I highly recommend investing in these extras.

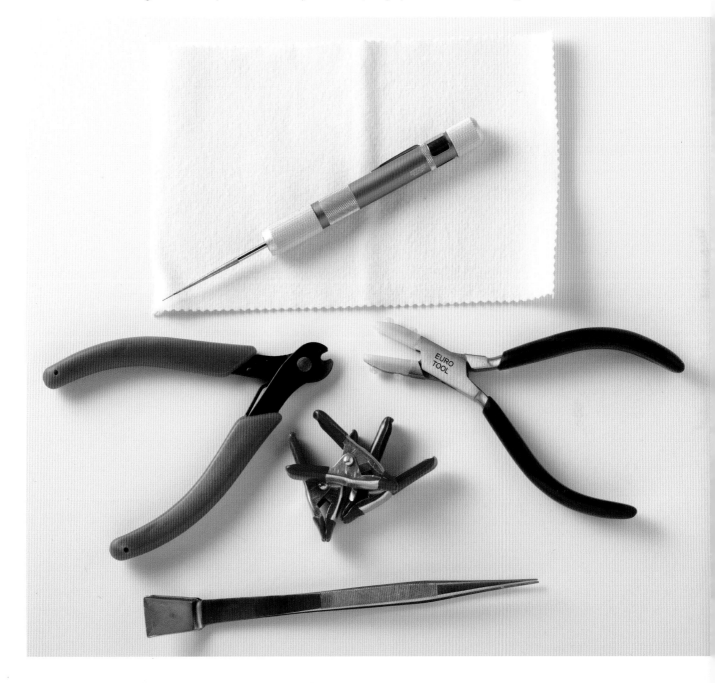

Toolbox extras like a polishing cloth, bead reamer, memory wire cutters, extra end clamps, and bead tweezers make beading faster and easier.

Bead reamer: If you have a bead that isn't drilled all the way through, a bead with something stuck inside it, or a bead with a hole that needs to be just a bit bigger, a bead reamer will save the day. A bead reamer comes with three interchangeable diamond-tip points that are stored in the handle when not in use. Using one of the tips, you can drill and smooth out almost any rough spots you may encounter in troublesome beads.

Bead tweezers: Bead tweezers are much longer than regular tweezers and come with a bead shovel at the end. The tips are useful for separating out individual beads from a collection for your design, while the opposing shovel end helps when you need to get lots of beads out of a bead storage box all at once. And, when the unavoidable bead spill happens, the shovel end will make cleanup a snap!

Jewelry glue: Jewelry glue is formulated specifically for the beads and metals that are used in jewelry making. The glue applicator is long and needle-like, allowing you to apply the glue in tiny areas. A little bit goes a long way with this extra-powerful adhesive.

Suzann's Sensational Beading Tip

Place a drop of water on a bead where you plan to drill it with the bead reamer. It will often make the reaming process easier.

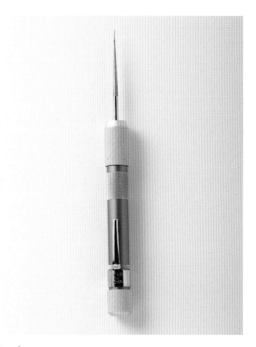

Bead reamer

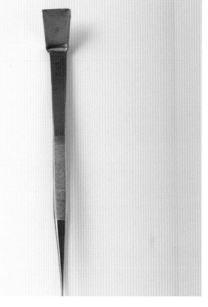

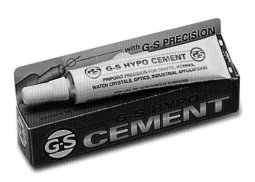

Jewelry glue. Photo supplied by Euro Tool, Inc.

Bead tweezers

Memory-wire cutters

Task lamp. Photo supplied by Euro Tool, Inc.

Polishing cloth

Memory wire cutters: Memory wire cutters are specially made to cut the super-strong steel wire that gives memory wire its name. These are the only cutters you should ever use to cut this wire. Using regular wire cutters on memory wire will destroy the cutting blades.

Polishing cloth: Metal findings can often lose their shine because of wear and tarnish, but a good polishing cloth can make your findings look brand new. Polishing cloths are about five dollars and can be used until they are totally black from removing tarnish. I prefer the cloths to polishing creams or liquids, as these can damage the porous surfaces of opals and pearls.

Suzann's Sensational Beading Tip

If you use reading glasses, I highly recommend keeping them on hand when you are designing jewelry. Not only will you be able to see the small beads and crimps you need to make your designs, you will be able to bead longer with less eye fatigue.

Task lamp: As a jewelry maker, you will need a well-lit area where you can complete your beading projects. Eventually, you may want to invest in a task lamp. Task lamps enable you to see the true color of your beads. Take it from personal experience, there is nothing worse than thinking you are beading with black beads, only to discover they are actually purple! My favorite task lamp is one that has a magnifier attached, giving you an extra bonus.

2

All About Beads

When walking into a bead store or down the beading aisle of your local craft superstore, the first thing you will notice is the overwhelming variety of beads. All those bold colors, textures, shapes, and sizes are enough to make your head swim. This chapter introduces you to the different types of beads and explains how to shop for them. Soon you will be able to make your bead choices like a pro!

You are never limited when it comes to bead selection. Beads are produced around the world in all imaginable colors and shapes using countless materials. With all the different options to explore, you can let your creativity run wild.

Where To Find Beads

If you've never been bead shopping before, the number of resources available might surprise you. While your local craft store is sure to be chock full of bead choices, you can also find special and unique beads at independent bead stores, antique shops, and more.

Antique, resale, and thrift stores, garage sales, and flea markets: These places might not be on the top of your list when searching for beads, but they are definitely worth a look. Often, you can take apart finished pieces of jewelry and end up with offbeat pendants, uniquely colored beads, and unusual clasps. The bonus is that you can usually get these remarkable items for fantastic prices.

Bead shows: Bead shows come in to metropolitan areas a few times a year. The variety and amount of beads that accompany them can be dizzying. Keep in mind that most shows only carry beads by the strand or in bulk. When you are buying that many beads at once, it is easy to quickly spend a lot of money. Setting a budget before arriving at the show can help you avoid overspending.

Suzann's Sensational Beading Tip

Don't forget to go shopping in your own jewelry collection. Many of us have necklaces, earrings, and bracelets lying in the depths of our jewelry box just waiting for a fresh new look! Rummage through your collection and you might find an outdated piece into which you can breathe new life.

Craft superstores: Beading has become so popular that most craft superstores now have fairly extensive beading sections. These aisles should provide you with a large variety of beads, findings, and tools for purchase. The beads at craft superstores are sold prepackaged or by the strand.

Independent bead stores: Your local independent bead shop can be a very encouraging place to look for beads and tools. The staff is usually well educated and willing to help you with any questions you may have. Beads at an independent bead store are typically sold individually and by the strand.

Internet sites: The Internet has brought us a plethora of beading sites. You can order beads from halfway across the world or from down the street. The benefit of Internet bead sites for jewelry makers is the variety of items they offer. The disadvantage is you are unable to view the beads in person. There is always a possibility that what appeared on your screen looks a lot different than what arrives in the mail!

Suzann's Sensational Beading Tip

When attending a bead show, you may want to bring a wheeled bag in which you can carry your purchases. Glass, stones, and metal, when bought in large quantities, can become quite heavy. Your back and arms will thank you!

Types of Beads

Beads come in all shapes, sizes, and colors. One of the joys of beading is that you get to explore and experiment with all of them. As you create your own projects, you'll quickly learn to what kinds of beads you are drawn. Here are some of the beads you're sure to come across as you design and work on your jewelry.

Ceramic beads: Ceramic beads are made out of clay and baked at high temperatures. The glazes used to color these beads range from muted to metallic. Ceramic beads come in many shapes and sizes, because they are often handmade. Exercise a bit of caution when handling these beads, because ceramics, although sturdy, can chip or break.

Ceramic beads

Czech glass: Bohemia, a region in the Czech Republic, has been known for its glass beads for thousands of years. Czech glass bead makers are true artisans who create a dazzling array of beads, often using a technique known as fire polishing. This means glazing in a hot oven, which smoothes out the rough edges created when the beads are machine faceted, polishing the beads.

Fair trade beads: The beads you buy not only make your jewelry beautiful, but they can also help the planet become a more beautiful place. The proceeds from the sale of Thai Hill Tribe silver beads help villagers in Thailand sustain their way of life. The organization Beads of Hope Africa helps Ugandan women out of poverty and improves the environment at the same time by teaching the women to make beads out of recycled paper. There are several other fair trade organizations through which you can purchase beads to support a good cause. One bead can change the world!

Czech glass beads

Fair trade beads

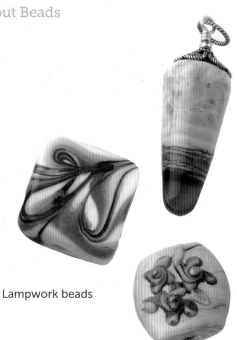

Lampwork beads

Lampwork beads: These glass handmade beads can be absolutely stunning. To create the beads, a glass bead maker sits in front of a torch (lamp), where he or she melts glass rods around a metal mandrel. Each bead is an individual work of art.

Natural beads: Some of the earliest beads ever discovered were made from natural materials. Natural beads can be made out of shell, bone, horn, wood, nuts, seeds, and various other naturally occurring materials. Many of these beads are porous and can be dyed in a myriad of colors. They can give a natural and earthy feel to jewelry. If you are looking for a lightweight material to work with, natural beads are a wonderful choice.

Suzann's Sensational Beading Tip

When looking for beads and earring findings, don't be thrown off by packets with metric measurements on them. All beads and earring findings are measured using the metric system, because many of them are produced overseas.

Pearls: Today, pearls are more popular than ever. Once known only for their round shape and white hue, pearls are now available in a variety of shapes, colors, and materials. Most pearls on the market today are freshwater pearls that come from farms. The farmers place a tiny "seed" into oysters to create the pearls. Other types of pearls are made out of glass and pressed shells.

Natural beads

Pearls

Pendants and focal beads: Pendants and focal beads are the stars of the show in jewelry making. Stunning focal beads are meant to catch the eye and draw attention to your fantastic jewelry composition.

Plastic beads: Before you skip this paragraph because you are remembering those plastic craft beads from your younger years, let me assure you that things have changed! Plastic beads now come in so many shapes and sizes you might find yourself touching them to make sure they are actually made out of plastic. One of the biggest benefits of plastic beads is that they are lightweight. They can be a terrific way to counter balance other beads that might cause a design to be too heavy.

Polymer clay: Polymer clay is actually a mixture of polyvinyl chloride (PVC) and liquid plasticizer and contains no clay at all. Regardless of its name, polymer clay is easy to sculpt into various shapes and forms. It comes in a wide range of colors, including some that glow in the dark. Different colors of polymer clay can be blended together to create custom hues. If you're feeling adventurous, try making your own polymer clay beads at home. The process is so easy, even a novice is sure to have success.

Pendants

Plastic beads

Polymer clay and beads

Seed beads: Those tiny little beads that you often see incorporated in weaving or embroidery are called seed beads. Made out of glass, the highest quality seed beads are produced in Japan. Seed beads come in various cuts, including bugles, hex cuts, cubes, and three cuts. When looking at the size listing on a package of seed beads, the bigger the number, the smaller the beads.

Swarovski crystals

Seed beads

Semi-precious gemstones: Semi-precious stones come in almost any color and shape you can imagine. These beads are made from stones mined all over the world. Beautiful purple amethyst, deep blue lapis lazuli, black sand onyx, and orange fire quartz are just some of the varieties available. New types of semi-precious stones will sometimes appear on the market due to shifts in the earth's crust or increased mining in a specific area. Pricing for semi-precious beads varies, depending on the number of imperfections present, how the beads are cut, the intensity of the color, how much the beads weigh, and the rarity of the stones from which the beads were cut.

Swarovski crystals: These amazing crystals are manufactured at the Swarovski factory in the Austrian Alps. Nothing shines quite like these crystals, so be careful of similar products that lack the Swarovski quality.

Semi-precious gemstones

Vintage beads

Vintage beads: When it comes to beads, the old adage, "they don't make them like they used to," can often ring true. The colors and materials popular in bygone eras can make for a distinctively unique piece. Utilizing vintage beads in jewelry is also a great way to go green with your designs, since you are reusing and recycling what has already been made.

Being mindful about metals

Metal beads and spacers are an alluring way to bring extra elegance or a little bit of edge to a piece of jewelry. When choosing metal beads, keep the following information in mind:

Base metal: Base metal is generally made of a mix of metals. This material is less expensive than other beads and can be a good choice for new jewelry makers. A problem with base metal is there is no way to know what metals were mixed to create it or what percentage of the finished product they represent. Because of this variation, base metals can have differing degrees of stiffness and flexibility.

Base metal beads

Brass and copper: With precious metal prices on the rise, jewelry makers have sought to use less expensive types of metal in their designs. As a result, copper and brass have both recently grown more popular. Both metals give an earthy feel to a piece when used in their natural states. For a vintage feel, antiqued copper and brass will fit your jewelry design perfectly.

Brass and copper beads

Gold beads

Gold-filled and gold-plated beads:
Gold-filled beads are made of a gold alloy that runs throughout the bead. Gold-plated beads, although cheaper than their gold-filled counterparts, have a gold finish that can eventually rub off from frequent wear.

Pewter beads

Pewter: During the creation of this book, sterling silver prices reached an all-time high. A more affordable alternative on the market is pewter. A mixture of metals, pewter is made from tin combined with copper or antimony to make it harder. In the past, pewter had a bad name because it contained lead. Modern pewter now contains antimony or bismuth instead of lead. Pewter also resists tarnishing for a much longer period than sterling silver.

Sterling silver: When it comes to sterling silver, you get what you pay for. If someone offers you beads in a silver tone at a cheap price and claims they are sterling silver, they probably aren't. You can double check the beads by looking for a stamp or marking on the packaging that reads 925, which indicates 92.5 percent of the metal is made of pure silver.

Sterling silver beads

Bead Shapes

Bead shapes are almost as varied as the countless colors and hues in which they are available. Here is a handy guide to many of the bead shapes you can find.

Bicone: This bead looks like two multi-faceted cones attached at the base. Bicones are most commonly identified with glass crystals, but other materials can also be found in this shape.

Briolette: This is a faceted teardrop-shaped bead. Often the hole is drilled across the top of the bead (horizontally), as opposed to straight up and down (vertically) through the bead.

Chip: These beads are small chips of stone with a hole drilled in the center. Chips can give a very organic and natural feel to a jewelry piece.

Bicones

Chip beads

Briolettes

Donuts

Coins

Cubes

Beads with filigree

Coin: Coins have a circular shape that can be either flat or slightly puffed. Pearls in a coin shape can be especially stunning.

Cube: The shape of this bead is like a cube with six equal square sides (think of a die from a board game). When you are making your jewelry, incorporate cubes for strong geometric designs.

Donut: Yes, just as the name implies, these beads do look like your favorite breakfast treat. They are typically circular, flat, and have a large hole in the center. Donuts are usually used as pendants because they are generally a larger cut of bead.

Filigree: When metal jewelry components have a lace-like look to them, this is called filigree. You can find filigree components on both beads and findings. When you want your jewelry to have a more formal or vintage appearance, filigree will help you obtain that look.

Heishi beads

Nuggets

Rondelles

Heishi: (Pronounced hee-shee.) Associated with necklaces popular during the 1960s and 1970s, Heishi beads are small round disks with flat edges. They are available in both semi-precious stones and metal. You can include them in your jewelry pieces by using them as spacers between beads or stack them together for a more dramatic effect. Heishi beads are a great choice when designing for men, because of their understated qualities.

Nugget: These "lumps of stone" beads are non-uniform in shape, with lots of bumps. The nugget shape can highlight the natural veins that run through a stone. It is a shape that will definitely be noticed when incorporated in your jewelry composition.

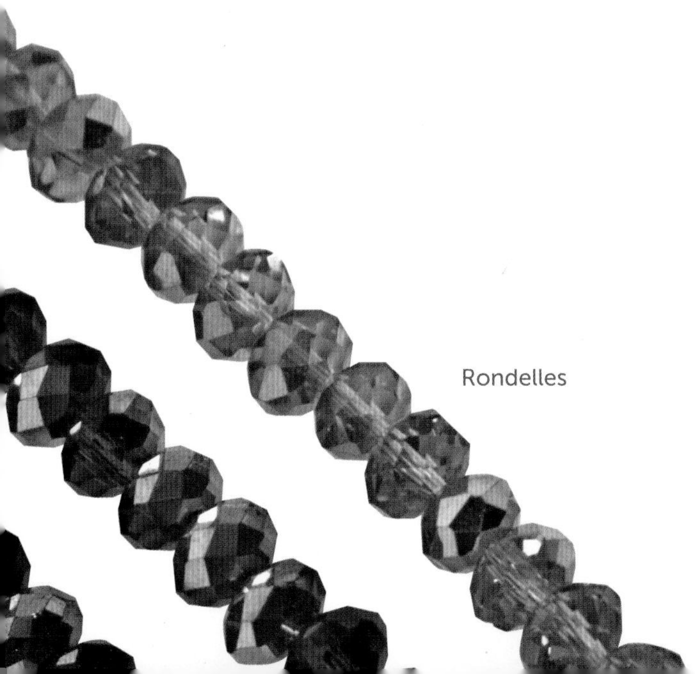

Rondelle: Rondelles may look familiar, since they are shaped like a tire or a round bead that has been pushed in on the sides. Spacers commonly come in this shape. Rondelles that are textured can give your jewelry that little bit of visual interest without being overwhelming.

3

Keeping It Together

While beads and pendants will typically be the most visible parts of your jewelry designs, the materials used to string and hold your beads together are just as important. Stringing materials such as wire, cord, and ribbon, and findings like clasps and eye pins, are the building blocks of any jewelry creation. You will come to find each of these stringing materials adds its own special touch to each jewelry design.

Jewelry creation is not limited to selecting and arranging beads. You can get creative with your use of beading wire, ribbon, and clasps to add a special touch to any project.

Stringing Materials

When you create a piece of jewelry, don't overlook the materials you are using to string your beads. Stringing materials like leather, ribbon, and chain can serve as decorative embellishments in a jewelry design, and portions of beading wire left exposed between beads adds a special ornamental touch. Feel free to experiment to see how different stringing materials can change the look of your designs.

Chain: Although you cannot technically string beads on chain, it has become a staple of jewelry design. You can buy it pre-packaged, have it cut to a specific length from a spool, or purchase the entire spool. Chain is now available in a variety of metals, shapes, sizes, and finishes. The links come soldered, meaning they are one solid piece, or unsoldered, meaning each link has a single cut, similar to a jump ring. Soldered links are great when you need one solid continuous circle, but you will lose a link or two when cutting it. You can easily adjust the length of an unsoldered chain by twisting open a link and removing a segment of chain. Make sure all links on an unsoldered chain are closed properly, as there is always the chance that one could be pulled open. There are two different ways to incorporate chain into your jewelry designs. First, you can use eye pins to create beaded links that can be connected to a premade chain or to other beaded links. Second, you can link eye pins together to create your own chain.

Chains

Suzann's Sensational Beading Tip

Flexible beading wire now comes in a wide variety of colors that can enhance your jewelry when exposed in your designs or when seen through clear beads.

Flexible beading wire:

Flexible beading wire really is the backbone of your jewelry designs. You will use it to string your beads for the vast majority of your necklace and bracelet creations. Flexible beading wire is made of strands of steel woven together and covered with a nylon coating. You can find it woven in 7-, 19-, 21-, or 49-strand counts. The higher the strand count, the more flexible the wire and the more expensive it is. Flexible beading wire comes in a variety of thicknesses. Fine wire (0.010" or 0.25mm in diameter) works well with pearls and other beads with small holes, while thicker wire (0.024" or 0.61mm) can be used for heavy beads. I recommend Soft Flex brand's medium 0.019" (0.48mm)/21-strand in original satin silver. Since the wire has a medium thickness, it will fit through the holes in almost all of your beads. Its flexibility will allow your jewelry to lie beautifully. Some brands of beading wire are labeled Good, Better, and Best. This is just another way of describing the thread count of the wire. You will see I have chosen to list thread count to describe the wire I used to create the projects in Chapter 5 (page 52). Ask the sales staff at your local craft superstore if you need help matching the wire I utilized to a wire brand that does not include the thread count on the label.

Flexible beading wire

Leather, cord, and ribbon: When you want to give your jewelry a unique and different feel, try incorporating leather, cord, or ribbon into your designs. Ribbon can bring a decidedly feminine feel to a jewelry piece, while leather is a great option when designing for men. All of these elements can be introduced into your jewelry with the use of fold-over crimps.

Leather, ribbon, and cord

Using Leather and Ribbon

Collect flat-nose pliers, scissors, a bead mat, jump rings, leather, cord, or ribbon, folded crimp ends, a clasp, beads of choice, and jewelry glue (optional). Cut your leather, cord, or ribbon to the length you desire. String your beads as you would like them. Once you are satisfied with your design, take one end of the material and lay it inside the open folded crimp. Gently bend one half of the folded crimp over the end of the leather, cord, or ribbon using your flat-nose pliers. Bend the second half of the folded crimp over the first half using the flat-nose pliers. Repeat with the other end of your necklace or bracelet. Attach jump rings to the loops at the tops of the folded crimps. Use the jump rings to attach your clasp.

Memory wire

Memory wire: Memory wire is made out of coiled stainless steel that maintains its round shape. Memory wire is most commonly found in bracelet size, but can also be purchased in ring and necklace sizes. Memory wire is an excellent choice for bracelets because it will fit any wrist. It wraps around the arm, and does not need a clasp. Memory wire should only be cut with memory wire cutters, as the wire's stiff stainless steel will destroy regular cutters.

Stretch wire/elastic cord: Stretch wire is used to make slip-on bracelets or necklaces without clasps. The cord is tied in a knot and dabbed with jewelry glue to finish the design. These pieces can stretch out over time and you should avoid using sharp beads that can eventually cut through the elastic cord.

Stretch wire

Make an Elastic Cord Bracelet

Elastic cord bracelets are simple and quick to make, and require no special techniques. You will need wire cutters, an end clamp, a bead mat, jewelry glue, elastic cord, and beads of your choice

Using your wire cutters, cut a length of elastic cord that is at least 4" (102mm) longer than the measurement of your wrist. Place an end clamp at one end of the cord and string on your beads. Once you are finished stringing your beads, remove the end clamp. Take both ends of the cord and make a square knot. Dab a small amount of jewelry glue on the knot to secure it. Cut off the excess elastic cord.

Jewelry Findings

Along with beads and stringing material, your jewelry pieces will also need findings. Findings are additional elements used to make a piece of jewelry. They can be functional, serving to connect, close, or fasten your jewelry, or decorative, adding a unique special touch.

Necklace and bracelet findings

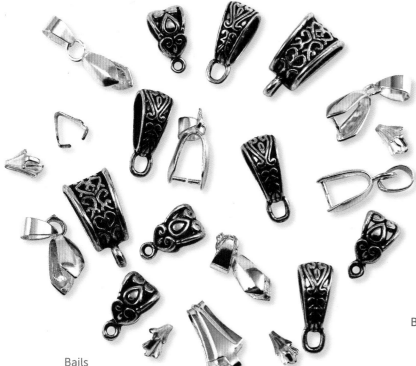

Bails

There are many different varieties of clasps and other findings you will need to use in your jewelry designs, and almost all of them can serve an ornamental, as well as a functional, purpose.

Barrel clasps

Bails: Do you have a pendant that only has one hole drilled through it at the top? A bail is what is attached to the pendant to enable it to hang from a necklace. A bail can be anything from a simple jump ring to a decorative piece that both hangs and enhances the pendant.

Barrel clasp: A barrel clasp has two pieces that are screwed together to make a closure. These were once a popular alternative for lobster claw clasps. Unfortunately, barrel clasps have a tendency to become undone on their own and should be used with caution.

Bead caps: Make your beads extra special by adding bead caps. These metal components are shaped like half a globe and are designed to partially cover a bead. Not only do they embellish your beads, they also prevent them from rubbing against each other.

Bead cones: Multi-strand necklaces and bracelets will often use cones in their designs as a decorative way to cover the place where all the strands come together. Cones are usually made out of metal, although recently ceramic cones have become available. Ceramic cones come in many different colors and patterns and can complement your jewelry design.

Box or tab clasp: Some of the most adorned and elaborate clasps are box or tab clasps. This closure is made by inserting a tab into a box-like shape. Some box clasps include a safety mechanism that prevents the tab from accidentally coming out.

Cones

Box clasps

Bead caps

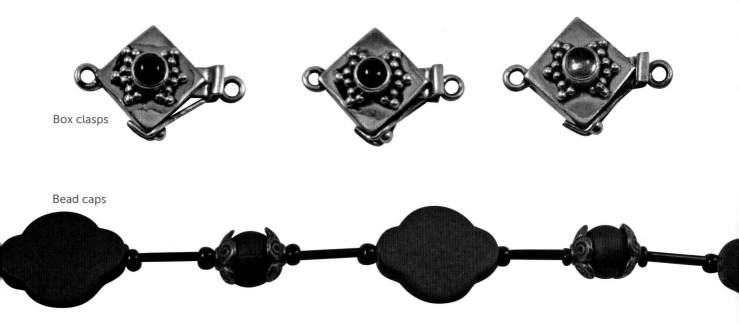

Crimp tubes

Crimp tubes: Crimp tubes, sometimes referred to as crimps, are small metal tubes with thin walls that are used on flexible beading wire to attach clasps and finish designs. When you go to purchase crimps, you will find both crimp tubes and crimp beads. I recommend using crimp tubes over crimp beads because they give crimping pliers a large surface area to grip. Purchase a pack of 2 x 2mm crimp tubes that are either gold filled or sterling silver. You might see crimp tubes available in base metal, but you will find sterling silver or gold-filled tubes crimp more easily and the results are more consistent. It is well worth it to pay a few extra pennies for quality crimp tubes that will keep your designs intact.

Folded crimp ends: Making jewelry with leather, cord, or ribbon can be fun, and folding crimp ends make attaching a clasp a breeze. A folding crimp has a loop at one end, enabling you to use a jump ring to attach a clasp or to crimp a section of beading wire to serve as a clasp loop. Add a dab of jewelry glue to the inside of a folding crimp to be sure your leather, cord, or ribbon stays in place.

Folded crimps

Hook and eye clasps

Hook and eye clasp: One half of this clasp consists of one piece that looks like an oversized J, while the other half is a ring or loop. The J piece is hooked onto the ring to close the clasp. The best use of hook and eye clasps is in necklaces. There might not be enough tension in a bracelet to keep a hook and eye clasp closed.

Jump rings: These metal rings have a cut on one side and are multi-purpose connecters used in jewelry making. Jump rings can be used to hang a pendant, connect links in bracelets and necklaces, and attach a clasp.

Lobster claw: These clasps are named for their close resemblance to a lobster claw. The "claw" mechanism is usually latched on to a jump ring, a link of chain, or another open loop to close a necklace or bracelet. These clasps are the most secure closures available, but because of their sturdy construction, the lever on the clasp can be difficult to open and close by the person wearing the jewelry.

Jump rings

Lobster clasp

Using a Jump Ring

It is very important that you learn to open and close a jump ring properly, or it can lose its shape and come apart later. You will need round-nose pliers, chain-nose pliers, and a jump ring.

Open the jump ring

Step 1: Take the chain-nose pliers in your left hand and, using the jaws, pick up your jump ring on the left-hand side close to the opening so that the opening is facing up.

Step 2: In your right hand, pick up the round-nose pliers and grasp the right side of the jump ring near the opening with the jaws. The jump ring should be now held by both sets of pliers.

Step 3: Slowly twist the sides of the jump ring in opposite directions to open it, one hand with the pliers moving forward and the other backward. The key is to twist, not pull. If a jump ring is pulled apart, the circle of the metal will become misshapen and will not close properly.

Close the jump ring

Step 1: Place the pliers back on either side of the opening and twist the ends back toward the center, letting them pass each other just a little bit.

Step 2: Twist the ends back to the center. You will know the jump ring is properly closed when you feel the two ends rub together or hear a little click. You may have to wiggle back and forth a few times and push the two sides in slightly with the pliers while the ends are passing one another to get the jump ring completely closed.

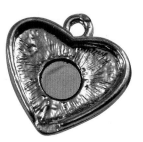

Magnetic clasps

S-hook clasps

Toggle clasp

Magnetic clasp: Using magnets to keep the two parts of the clasp together, a magnetic clasp is easy to open and close and comes in a wide variety of styles. The magnets can be demagnetized over time, however, causing your clasp to fall apart. Because the magnets are often tiny, these clasps should not be incorporated in jewelry for small children, since they are a choking hazard. Magnets can also affect electronic equipment, such as a pacemaker. Avoid giving jewelry with magnetic clasps to individuals with health problems who might be required to use a pacemaker or other similar equipment.

S-hook clasp: This clasp is similar to a hook and eye clasp, except one half is shaped like an *s* instead of a *J*. The clasp is closed by slipping one of the curves of the S through a jump ring, ring, or loop. S-hook clasps are best for necklaces, since the weight of the jewelry creates tension to keep the clasp closed. Many S-hook clasps are quite ornate. Consider using them as a decorative element when designing your jewelry.

Toggle clasp: Toggle clasps are one of the most popular and simplest closures for necklaces and bracelets. They consist of two pieces, a bar and a loop. The bar is put through the loop and laid flat to close a jewelry piece. When choosing a toggle, make sure the bar portion overlaps the loop far enough so the toggle will not slip apart.

Chandeliers

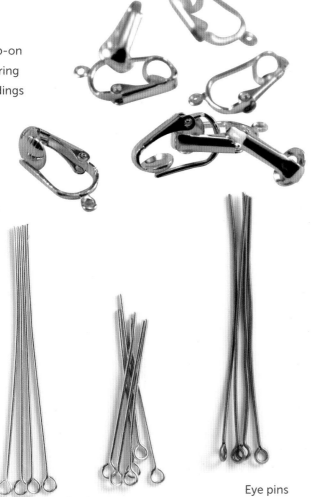

Clip-on earring findings

Earring findings

Chandeliers: Add an extra bit of elegance to your earrings by using chandeliers. These earring findings are used for dangling designs, letting beads swing and move freely. They are perfect for individuals with long necks.

Clip-ons: These are not your grandmother's clip-ons. Today's designs are styled in such a way that they look like earrings created for pierced ears. Many clip-ons now come with adjustable tension, allowing the wearer to personalize the fit, keeping her ears from feeling pinched.

Eye pins: Eye pins look similar to straight sewing pins, but have a loop on one end. This loop allows you to hang beaded units from a pendant or the main part of an earring design. A simple way to make your own beaded chain is to link eye pins together and attach a clasp.

Eye pins

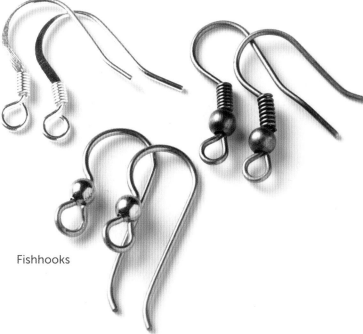

Fishhooks

Fishhooks: Sometimes called French wires, these findings have a hook-like shape. They are best used with a plastic nut, which is slipped onto the hook after the earring has been put in place to make sure it does not fall out.

Head pins: Head pins look similar to straight sewing pins with the sharp part cut off. They can have either flat or decorative bottoms, which are used to keep beads from falling off your earring. They come in every type of metal available on the market.

Hoops: If you want to make a statement with your earrings, hoops will definitely stand out. They can be plain or shaped as semi-circles, from which you can dangle beads. Plain hoops can also be turned into beaded wine charms.

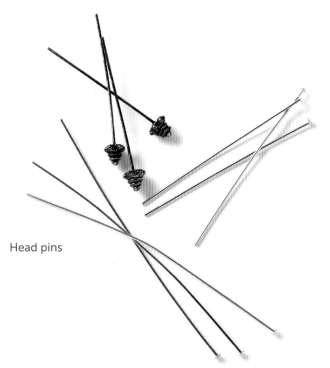

Head pins

Hoops

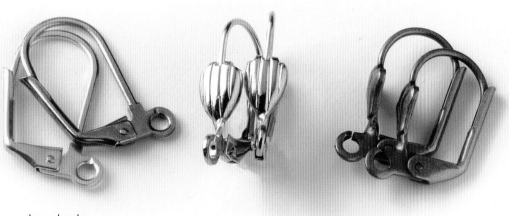

Leverbacks

Posts

Leverbacks: Similar in design to fishhooks, these findings have a lever in the back used to close them completely, assuring you that your earring won't fall out. Leverbacks will quickly become one of your favorite earring findings.

Posts: Posts, sometimes referred to as studs, consist of a straight post that is inserted though the ear and secured by a backing or nut. At one time, posts only had a plain ball at the front. Today, posts can have many different motifs to enhance the look of your earrings. Posts can be especially beneficial when you want to make shorter earrings.

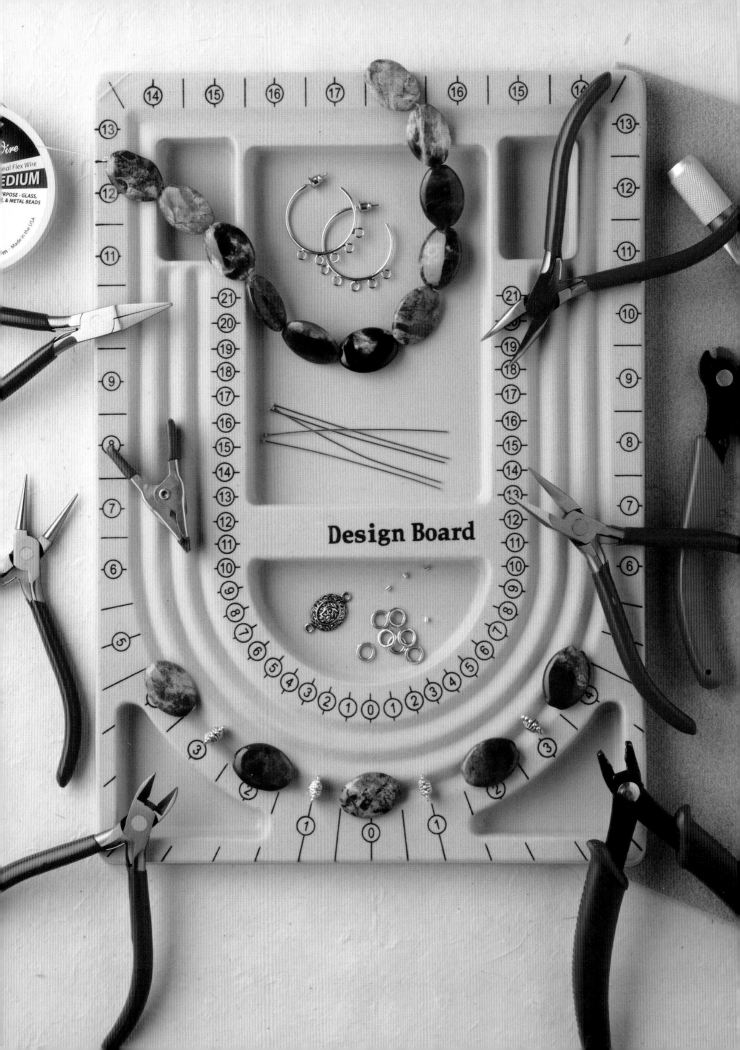

A Jewelry Maker's
Shopping List

Tools

- ❏ Bead board
- ❏ Bead mat
- ❏ Bent-nose pliers
- ❏ Crimping pliers
- ❏ End clamps
- ❏ Flat-nose pliers
- ❏ Chain-nose pliers
- ❏ Round-nose pliers
- ❏ Wire cutters

Earring-making Supplies

- ❏ Beads
- ❏ Earring findings
- ❏ Eye pins (if making dangling earrings)
- ❏ Head pins

Bracelet- and Necklace-making Supplies

- ❏ Beads
- ❏ Clasps
- ❏ Head pins or eye pins (if making your own pendant)
- ❏ Nylon-coated beading wire of medium diameter in 19- or 21-strand count
- ❏ 2 x 2mm crimps; either gold filled or sterling silver

Optional Items

- ❏ Bead reamer
- ❏ Bead tweezers
- ❏ Jewelry glue
- ❏ Memory wire
- ❏ Memory wire cutters
- ❏ Polishing cloths
- ❏ Task lamp

Beader's FAQs

What are the birthstones for each month of the year, and what are the colors if I want to design a piece using glass crystals?

This chart reflects the jewelry industry standard for the modern birthstone calendar.

Birthstone Calendar

Month	Gemstone	Birthstone color
January	Garnet	Deep red
February	Amethyst	Purple
March	Aquamarine or bloodstone	Pale blue
April	Diamond	Clear or crystal
May	Emerald	Green
June	Pearl, moonstone, or alexandrite	White
July	Ruby	Bright or true red
August	Peridot	Pale green
September	Sapphire or lapis lazuli	Deep blue
October	Opal or pink tourmaline	Multi-colored or pink
November	Yellow topaz or citrine	Yellow
December	Blue topaz, turquoise, or tanzanite	Bright or true blue

How many beads will fit per inch of wire?

Approximate Number of Beads to Inches of Wire

Bead size	Beads per inch (25mm)	7" (178mm)	16" (406mm)	24" (610mm)	32" (813mm)	36" (914mm)
3mm	8.25	57	132	200	265	288
4mm	6.25	43	100	150	200	225
5mm	5	35	82	124	160	180
6mm	4.25	28	67	100	132	153
7mm	3.5	24	57	85	114	126
8mm	3.25	22	50	75	100	112
10mm	2.5	18	40	60	80	90
12mm	2	15	33	50	66	72
14mm	1.75	13	29	43	56	63
16mm	1.5	11	25	38	50	54
18mm	1.25	10	23	34	45	50
20mm	1.2	8	20	29	38	43

Bead Size Chart

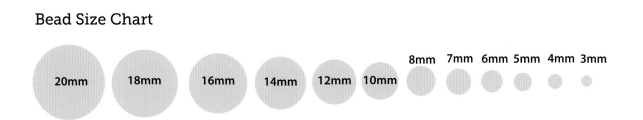

What are standard bracelet and necklace lengths?

Bracelet Measurements

Size	Length (US)	Length (Metric)
Children	5–6"	127–152mm
Women	7–7½"	178–191mm
Men	8–9"	203–229mm

There are various lengths that are considered "standard" when designing jewelry. When designing jewelry for others, you must remember that every person is different, so the following measurements are merely guidelines. You may have to adjust the sizing to fit yourself or the lucky individual who will receive your gift.

Necklace Measurements

Name	Description	Length (US)	Length (Metric)
Children's	About the size of a choker	14–16"	356–406mm
Men's	About the size of a matinee or opera necklace	18–20"	457–508mm
Women's collar	Fits directly at the neck	12–13"	305–330mm
Choker	Lies at the base of the neck	14–16"	356–406mm
Princess	Lies near the collarbone	18"	457mm
Matinee	Lies near the bust	20–24"	508–610mm
Opera	Lies at the breastbone	30–36"	762–914mm
Rope	Can be very long; worn as a single strand or in several loops around the neck	Over 36"	Over 914mm

What questions should I ask if I am making jewelry for someone else?

Once you start making and wearing lots of your own fabulous jewelry, people will start to notice. Soon you will be asked to make necklaces, bracelets, and earrings for others. Whether it is a family member, your best friend, or a co-worker, here are some questions you may want to ask before you start designing their sensational work of wearable art.

1. Do you have a favorite color?
2. What colors do you wear most often?
3. Do you prefer silver or gold?
4. Are you allergic to any metals?
5. What length bracelet/necklace do you prefer? (If they don't know, ask them to measure their favorite piece of jewelry and let you know what the measurement is.)
6. Is this for a formal occasion or for everyday use?
7. Do you have a price range in which you would like to stay? Note: This is very important before purchasing the materials for this project.

4

Simple Steps to Making Jewelry

Now that you are well versed in all the tools, beads, and other jewelry-making materials you will need, it's time to put your knowledge into practice and try your hand at a few simple projects. Use the two step-by-step projects in this chapter to kick off your jewelry-making experience and hone your skills. In no time, you'll be ready to start making projects of your own

Just a handful of materials will get your jewelry-making process started. Remember that you can always make adjustments or substitutions to a project to make it suit your personal taste.

Simple Dangle Earrings

Gather together:

- ❑ Round-nose pliers
- ❑ Chain-nose pliers
- ❑ Wire cutters
- ❑ Bead mat
- ❑ Pair of earring findings (leverbacks, fish hooks, or posts)
- ❑ Head pins
- ❑ Beads of choice

1 Design your earrings. Arrange your beads on the head pin as you would like them. When adding your beads, remember to leave at least ½" (13mm) of the top of the head pin exposed so you can make a loop. When you're just starting out, you might find it easier to leave a longer length of the pin exposed, as shown here.

2 Bend the head pin. Using your chain-nose pliers, bend the exposed top of the head pin at a 90-degree angle, flush against the top bead of your design.

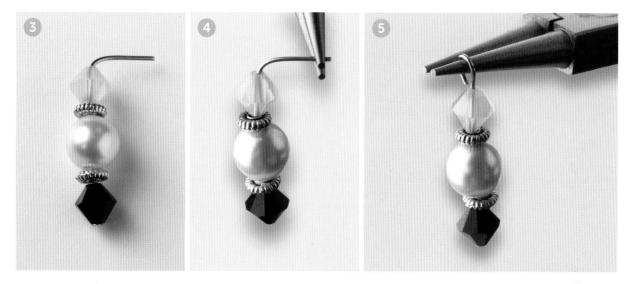

3 **Trim the head pin.** Cut the exposed head pin wire down to ¼" (6mm).

4 **Go "tip to tip."** Use the area close to the tip of your round-nose pliers to grasp the tip of the head pin.

5 **Form a loop.** Twist your wrist to roll up and over with your pliers to form a loop out of the tip of your head pin.

6 **Attach the finding.** Swing the loop open—don't pull. Attach your earring finding and swing the loop closed. Make sure the ends of your loop fit together tightly, so it does not fall off your earring finding.

7 **Make the second earring.** Repeat the previous steps with the remaining beads, head pin, and finding to make your second earring.

Suzann's Sensational Beading Tip

The twist of your wrist used to make a loop is very similar to that of turning a can opener.

Simple Bracelet or Necklace with Crimps

Tools:
- ❏ Crimping pliers
- ❏ Wire cutters
- ❏ Bead board
- ❏ Bead mat
- ❏ End clamp

Materials:
- ❏ Beading wire
- ❏ Clasp
- ❏ 2 x 2mm crimps
- ❏ Beads

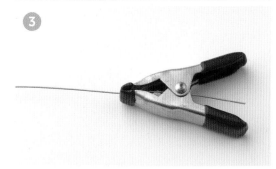

1 Arrange your beads. Organize your beads on a bead board to design your jewelry composition. Remember, the center of your design will always be at the number zero on the bead board. If using a multi-channel bead board, only use the outside track when measuring the piece. This will give you the correct measurement in inches.

2 Measure and cut the wire. Once you are happy with your design, take your beading wire and measure your design on the bead board. Add an additional 4" (102mm) to the total length of the wire and cut it. The extra wire will ensure you have enough at either end of your design when you are ready to attach your clasp.

3 Attach an end clamp. Place an end clamp 2" (51mm) from one end of the wire. The end clamp will keep your beads from falling off the wire while you are stringing them.

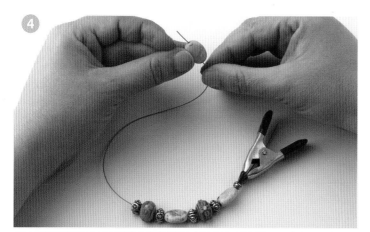

4 **String the beads.** String your beads onto the wire. You may want to lay your piece back down on the bead board once you have placed the beads. Designs can sometimes look different or be a different length once strung.

5 **String one crimp and half the clasp.** Once you are done stringing your last bead, string on one crimp tube. Next, string on one half of your clasp.

6 **Secure the clasp.** Feed the wire back through the crimp, pulling it tightly so the clasp is snugly held in the loop created by the wire. Make sure the crimp tube is flush against the last bead with no wire showing.

7 **Prepare to close the crimp tube.** Grab your crimping pliers. You will see two half circles located in the lower jaw. Position the pliers around the crimp tube, using the half circle that is closest to your hand.

8 **Make the first crimp.** Make sure the wires that are threaded through the crimp tube are not crossed. Squeeze the pliers firmly and then open the jaws. You should see two u-shaped channels in the crimp tube.

9 **Prepare for the second crimp.** Take the crimp tube and put it in the half circle of the crimping pliers that is furthest from your hand. Stand it up so that the two channels you just made are facing you.

10 **Make the second crimp.** Squeeze the pliers together so the crimp tube folds and the two channels in the tube meet.

11 **Trim the wire and finish.** Cut the wire tail as close to the crimp tube as possible with your wire cutters. Turn your design over to the unfinished end. Remove the end clamp and repeat steps 5–10 with the other half of the clasp.

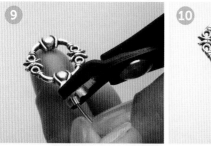

5

Jewelry Designs

Now that you've had some practice, you are ready to start making your own collection of fabulous jewelry creations. Use the designs in this chapter to make earrings, bracelets, and necklaces for yourself, your friends, and your family. Remember, you can always alter the designs to suit your taste and style, so don't be afraid to let your creativity run wild. These projects are just the beginning of what you can do with your creativity.

Memories of Margret, page 77.

Earrings

Earrings can be made in all different shapes, sizes, and colors. You can make a simple pair of posts to wear to work or make a colorful pair of dangle earrings to wear with your favorite dress. Get inspired by these designs to make a pair for every outfit and every occasion.

Suzann's Sensational Beading Tip

Have a question about one of the projects in this book? Contact Suzann at *suzann@beadphoria.com* for help and advice.

Merlot, anyone?

Make heads turn at your next dinner party with these earrings. The Swarovski Crystal dangles and Sterling Silver ovals will catch the eye of all the guests!

Tools

- ❏ Round-nose pliers
- ❏ Flat-nose pliers
- ❏ Wire cutters
- ❏ Bead mat

Materials

- ❏ 6 head pins
- ❏ 2 eye pins
- ❏ 2 sterling silver ovals
- ❏ 2 purple Lucite rondelle faceted beads
- ❏ Two 6mm fuchsia Swarovski crystal bicones
- ❏ Two 6mm purple velvet Swarovski crystal bicones
- ❏ Two 6mm tanzanite Swarovski crystal bicones

Tropical Sparkle

Bring the beach to you any time of the year with these Tropical Sparkle earrings. The turquoise, fire opal, and yellow colors will instantly bring you back to the surf, sun, and sand.

Tools

- ❑ Chain-nose pliers
- ❑ Round-nose pliers
- ❑ Bead mat
- ❑ Wire cutters

Materials

- ❑ 2 jump rings
- ❑ 12 silver-colored head pins
- ❑ 4 each 6mm Swarovski crystal bicones in turquoise, fire opal, and yellow
- ❑ 2 silver donut components
- ❑ 2 lengths of Rolo-style chain with 10 links each
- ❑ 2 fishhook earring findings

Very Tweet

By bringing the right components together, you can create earrings that are beautiful, yet extremely easy to make. This pair of earrings, using bird's nest components made by Emily of the Bead Bucket in Ephraim, Wisconsin, and fishhook ear wires, comes together in a flash. Note that you can substitute any unique bead you like for the Nesting Bird component.

Tools

❑ Chain-nose pliers
❑ Round-nose pliers
❑ Bead mat

Materials

❑ Fishhook earring findings
❑ 1 pair of the Nesting Bird components by Emily of the Bead Bucket in Ephraim, Wisconsin

Swing open the loop on the bottom of one of the fishhook earring findings using your round-nose and chain-nose pliers. Add one of the Nesting Bird components to the open loop. Swing the loop closed to complete the earring. Repeat for the second earring.

Natural Hoops

These earrings have a natural earthy style, perfect for a summer season outdoors.

Tools

- ❑ Chain-nose pliers
- ❑ Round-nose pliers
- ❑ Bead mat

Materials

- ❑ 2 hammered 14mm copper donuts
- ❑ 1 pair of 2" (51mm) copper eye pins
- ❑ Copper fishhook earring findings
- ❑ Two 11mm wooden Rudraksha beads
- ❑ Two 12mm ceramic aqua disks
- ❑ Four 8mm wooden rondelles

Using the chain-nose and round-nose pliers, swing open the bottom loop of one eye pin. Hook the eye pin through the hole on the top of the hammered copper donut. Swing the eye pin closed. Slide one wooden rondelle, one aqua ceramic disk, a second wooden rondelle, and one Rudraksha bead onto the eye pin. Make a simple loop at the top. Swing open the simple loop and attach it to one of the copper fishhooks. Repeat steps to complete second earring.

A Crystal Christmas

When these beads are combined, they form a Christmas tree complete with a star on top. They are a wonderfully sophisticated way to celebrate·the season—perfect as a gift for a friend or yourself.

Tools
- ❏ Flat-nose pliers
- ❏ Round-nose pliers
- ❏ Wire cutters
- ❏ Bead mat

Materials
- ❏ 1 pair silver ball post earring findings
- ❏ Two 2" (51mm) silver head pins
- ❏ Two 5 x 5mm double-sided stars in antique silver
- ❏ Two 10 x 14mm angelic crystal faceted tear drops in green
- ❏ Two 10mm angelic crystal faceted rondelles in brown

Slide one angelic crystal faceted rondelle in brown, one angelic crystal faceted teardrop in green, and one double-sided star in antique silver onto each head pin in that order. Make a simple loop at the top of each head pin. Swing open the simple loops and attach one to each of the silver ball post earring findings.

Bracelets

A bracelet is a great accessory to add to any outfit. Make a single-strand piece to wear with your favorite jeans and t-shirt ensemble. A glamorous multi-strand bracelet can become a great conversation piece if you're enjoying a night out. Add some extra length to a bracelet design, and you can easily wear it as an anklet.

Asian Blossoms

The delicate blooms on the lampwork beads of this bracelet are reminiscent of Japanese lanterns. Highlighting the colors using Swarovski crystals in fire opal and fuchsia, the bracelet is a beautiful addition to any wardrobe.

Tools

- ❏ Bead board
- ❏ Bead mat
- ❏ Crimping pliers
- ❏ Wire cutters

Materials

- ❏ 19-strand count beading wire in gold
- ❏ Two 2 x 2mm gold-filled crimp tubes
- ❏ One 15mm gold rose toggle clasp
- ❏ Two 4mm gold pewter spheres
- ❏ Ten 6mm gold pewter rondelles
- ❏ Six 6mm fire opal Swarovski crystal bicones
- ❏ Eight 6mm fuchsia Swarovski crystal bicones
- ❏ Five 14mm orange and fuchsia blossom rondelle glass lampwork beads

Desert Waters

Inspired by the colors of the southwestern United States, the mix of sandy colored desert flower beads and oval turquoise beads in this bracelet are like an oasis in a barren land.

Tools

❑ Bead board

❑ Bead mat

❑ Crimping pliers

❑ Wire cutters

Materials

❑ 21-strand count original beading wire

❑ Two 2 x 2mm sterling silver crimps

❑ One 18 x 17mm silver pewter decorated toggle

❑ Eight 4 x 6.5mm four circle corner silver pewter rondelle spacers

❑ Two 4.5 x 6mm bumpy silver pewter spacers

❑ Four 10 x 13mm desert flower lampwork beads

❑ Five 10 x 14mm oval turquoise beads

Metallic Shimmer

This stunning bracelet, made entirely of silver beads, is perfect for everyday wear. The various bead textures make what could be a boring monotone bracelet into a captivating piece.

Tools

❑ Bead board

❑ Bead mat

❑ Crimping pliers

❑ Wire cutters

Materials

❑ 19-strand count original beading wire

❑ Two 2 x 2mm sterling silver crimp tubes

❑ One 16mm silver toggle clasp

❑ Twelve 8mm silver spheres

❑ Four 10 x 8mm silver yin/yang oval beads

❑ Five 12 x 10 x 10mm silver bumpy box beads

Bountiful Harvest

Gold, orange, and yellow hues can help us recall the changing of the seasons. Observe the time when we give thanks by making this double-stranded bracelet.

Tools

❑ Bead board

❑ Bead mat

❑ Crimping pliers

❑ Wire cutters

Materials

❑ 19-strand count gold beading wire

❑ Four 2 x 2mm gold crimp tubes

❑ 1 double-strand oval gold clasp

❑ Four 6mm gold balls

❑ Thirteen 14mm amber foil glass lentil beads

❑ Eighteen 10 x 12mm fall-colored pumpkin-shaped dyed turquoise beads

Suzann's Sensational Beading Tip

When working with larger beads in a bracelet, make sure you leave a little wire exposed at the end before you crimp. This way your bracelet will have enough flexibility to bend around your wrist.

Abalone Reflections

Abalone shell beads, freshwater pearls, Swarovski crystals, and silver all have an inner reflective quality that is hard to resist. By combining all of these elements, you have a bracelet that is truly enchanting.

Tools

- ❏ Bead board
- ❏ Bead mat
- ❏ Crimping pliers
- ❏ Wire cutters

Materials

- ❏ 19-strand count original beading wire
- ❏ Two 2 x 2mm sterling silver crimp tubes
- ❏ 1 silver hook and eye clasp
- ❏ 4 abalone shell coins
- ❏ Six 6mm rosaline Swarovski crystal bicones
- ❏ Three cobalt blue center-drilled freshwater coin pearls
- ❏ Twelve 5mm silver bumpy round spacer beads

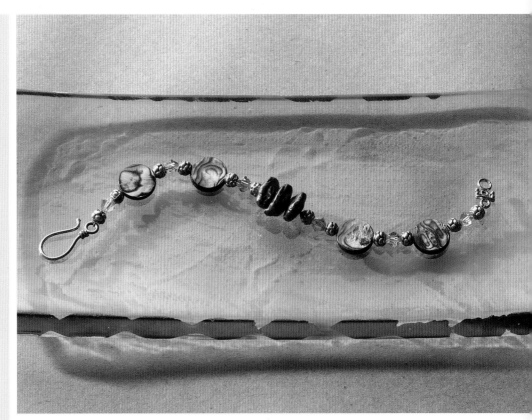

Violets & Sunshine

Have flowers and sunshine with you wherever you go. The purple, gold, and green tones in this piece are sure to bring a smile to your face every time you look at your wrist.

Tools

❑ Bead board

❑ Bead mat

❑ Crimping pliers

❑ Wire cutters

Materials

❑ 19-strand count gold beading wire

❑ Two 2 x 2mm gold-filled crimp tubes

❑ 1 gold pewter rose toggle clasp

❑ 14 gold daisy spacers

❑ Eight 6mm peridot Swarovski crystal bicones

❑ 3 lampwork flower beads

❑ 4 purple oval beads

Forest Sunrise

Looking for a bracelet that is quick to make, but still elegant and fashionable? The Forest Sunrise *bracelet incorporates stylish pre-made chain for a piece that can be completed in less than ten minutes!*

Tools
❏ Bead mat
❏ Round-nose pliers
❏ Wire cutters

Materials
❏ Chain
❏ 1 gold lobster claw clasp
❏ 1 jump ring
❏ One 2" (51mm) gold eye pin
❏ 1 agate square frame
❏ One 10 x 14mm oval turquoise bead

Lay the agate square frame on your bead mat. Place the oval turquoise bead in the center of frame so that the holes of the frame and the bead are aligned. Insert the eye pin through the holes of the frame and the bead. Make a loop out of the exposed eye pin wire (see the Simple Dangle Earrings project in Chapter 4). There should be two eye pin loops on either side of the frame: the original loop already made in the pin, and the one you just made. This piece will be the center unit for your bracelet. Swing open one of the eye pin loops on the center unit using the round-nose pliers. Attach the loop to a link of chain and close it again with round-nose pliers. Repeat this step with the other end of the eye pin. On one end of the unattached chain, connect the lobster claw clasp using the jump ring (see page 37). Use the last link on the other end of the chain as the other half of your clasp.

Spring Fling

Spring makes an appearance in this composition that melds soft pastels with strong greens and blues.

Tools

- ❑ Bead board
- ❑ Bead mat
- ❑ Crimping pliers
- ❑ Wire cutter

Materials

- ❑ 19-strand count original beading wire
- ❑ Two 2 x 2mm sterling silver crimp tubes
- ❑ 1 silver bumpy heart toggle clasp
- ❑ One 18mm flower power disk-shaped bead
- ❑ Eight 6mm round fire-polished Czech glass beads
- ❑ Six 14mm lampwork bumpy beads in coordinating colors
- ❑ Sixteen 3mm filigree silver beads

Vintage Time

This classy watch not only keeps you on time, but also brings a bit of bling to your wrist. The project also introduces a double strand. Don't be intimidated, a double strand is easy to make. When you start the project, cut two identical lengths of wire. Thread your beads onto both wires until you reach the point at which you'd like the double strand to begin. Then, thread beads onto only one wire at a time. When you want to go back to a single strand, start threading both wires through your beads once more.

Tools

- ❏ Bead board
- ❏ Bead mat
- ❏ Crimping pliers
- ❏ Wire cutters

Materials

- ❏ 19-strand count original beading wire
- ❏ Two 2 x 2mm sterling silver crimp tubes
- ❏ 1 silver antique flower toggle clasp
- ❏ 1 watch face in lilac
- ❏ Two 14mm amethyst Swarovski crystal silver double strand sliders
- ❏ Thirty-two 4mm lilac fire-polished Czech beads
- ❏ Six 8mm lilac fire-polished Czech beads

Necklaces

You can make a necklace of any length to suit what you are wearing. A choker will sit at the base of your neck, perfect for t-shirts, while a matinee necklace can add color to a business outfit. An exceptionally long rope necklace can be twisted and draped around your neck any way you want.

Blue Birds In Flight

A pendant designed by Lisa Petrillo of Lucid Moon Studio inspired this necklace. The blue coral teardrop-shaped beads remind me of feathers. They are the perfect touch to tie all the elements in this piece together.

Tools

❑ Bead Board
❑ Bead mat
❑ Crimping pliers
❑ Wire cutters

Materials

❑ 19-strand count original beading wire
❑ Six 2 x 2mm sterling silver crimp tubes
❑ 1 blue bird pendant
❑ 2 silver bird-shaped links
❑ 1 swirl toggle clasp
❑ Four 6mm crystal Aurora Borealis (AB) Swarovski crystals
❑ Twelve 8mm black onyx polished nuggets
❑ Two 8mm wooden decoupage beads
❑ Ten 5mm silver spacer discs

Round and Round Retro

Take a trip back to the 60s and 70s with this groovy motif.

Tools

- ❏ Bead board
- ❏ Bead mat
- ❏ Crimping pliers
- ❏ Wire cutters

Materials

- ❏ 19-strand count original beading wire
- ❏ Two 2 x 2mm sterling silver crimp tubes
- ❏ 1 silver hammered heart toggle clasp
- ❏ Twenty-eight 6mm Swarovski crystals in various colors
- ❏ 13 swirl coin beads
- ❏ Fourteen 4 x 6mm silver flower beads

Hollywood Glamor

The beauty of Hollywood's glory days is highlighted in this necklace, using vintage Swarovski crystals, rondelles, and pearls. One of the big screen's original divas, Marylyn Monroe, has a starring role in a pendant featuring an original drawing by Marin M. Rocha.

Tools

- ❏ Bead board
- ❏ Bead mat
- ❏ Crimping pliers
- ❏ Wire cutters

Materials

- ❏ 19-strand count original beading wire
- ❏ Two 2 x 2mm sterling silver crimp tubes
- ❏ 1 sterling silver with black onyx tab clasp
- ❏ 1 pendent with Marylyn Monroe drawing by Marin M. Rocha
- ❏ Eight 10mm off-white Swarovski pearls
- ❏ 8 vintage Swarovski crystals
- ❏ Ten 10mm helix Swarovski crystals
- ❏ Eight 8mm Swarovski crystal rondelles

Caramel Cappuccino

Yummy caramel, chocolate, and coffee colors swirl together to make this composition a treat for the eyes.

Tools

- ❏ Bead board
- ❏ Bead mat
- ❏ Crimping pliers
- ❏ Wire cutters

Materials

- ❏ 19-strand count original beading wire
- ❏ Four 2 x 2mm copper crimp tubes
- ❏ 1 copper toggle clasp
- ❏ 1 foiled glass oval focal
- ❏ Two 10 x 13mm oval copper links
- ❏ Two 26 x 12mm rectangular foiled glass beads
- ❏ Two 15mm copper metal flower beads
- ❏ Two 12mm copper metal bicone beads
- ❏ Eight 6mm tiger eye gemstone rounds
- ❏ Various accent beads in copper and brown tones

Global Harmony

The swirled greens and blues on the pendant and beads for this necklace are reminiscent of the view of the earth from space.

Tools

- ❑ Bead board
- ❑ Bead mat
- ❑ Crimping pliers
- ❑ Wire cutters

Materials

- ❑ 19-strand count original beading wire
- ❑ Two 2 x 2mm sterling silver crimp tubes
- ❑ Silver toggle clasp
- ❑ Ten 6mm silver round beads
- ❑ Two 16mm scrollwork silver beads
- ❑ Two pairs of 16mm silver bead caps
- ❑ Eighteen 16mm mosaic turquoise round beads
- ❑ Two 18 x 22mm tiger iron faceted nuggets
- ❑ Eighteen 5mm tiger iron chips
- ❑ One 30mm puffed oval mosaic turquoise pendant

Time Flies

You can make time stand still with this Steampunk-inspired necklace.

Tools

- ❏ Bead board
- ❏ Bead mat
- ❏ Crimping pliers
- ❏ Wire cutters

Materials

- ❏ 19-strand count original beading wire
- ❏ Two 2 x 2mm sterling silver crimp tubes
- ❏ 1 pendant from Earthenwood Studios
- ❏ Various coordinating vintage beads
- ❏ 1 large silver toggle clasp
- ❏ Two 12mm ceramic links from Earthenwood Studios

Little Miss America

This piece is perfect for a little Fourth of July pride.

Tools

- ❑ Bead board
- ❑ Bead mat
- ❑ Crimping pliers
- ❑ Wire cutters

Materials

- ❑ 19-strand count original beading wire
- ❑ Two 2 x 2mm sterling silver crimp tubes
- ❑ Silver heart toggle clasp
- ❑ Six 16mm blue and white bumpy glass beads
- ❑ Four 16mm blue, white, and light blue bumpy glass beads
- ❑ Forty-two 6mm silver daisy spacers
- ❑ Eight 15mm white coin-shaped freshwater pearls
- ❑ Eighteen 10mm Czech fire-polished glass beads
- ❑ White and blue glass lampwork dress pendant

It's Only Rock And Roll

Have fun with fashion! This necklace shows the world your love of great jewelry and classic rock and roll. Incorporating chain like the one used here into a project can be a great budget saver. A nice silver chain can be paired with a handful of expensive crystal beads to make a dazzling necklace at a bargain price.

Tools

- ☐ Bead board
- ☐ Bead mat
- ☐ Crimping pliers
- ☐ Wire cutters

Materials

- ☐ 19-strand count original beading wire
- ☐ Two 2 x 2mm sterling silver crimp tubes
- ☐ Gunmetal oval chain
- ☐ Rolling Stones bottle cap focal pendant
- ☐ Silver filigree toggle clasp
- ☐ Two 8mm wooden decoupage music beads
- ☐ Four 6mm daisy spacers
- ☐ Four 10mm jet Swarovski crystals
- ☐ Two 20 x 15mm dyed red shell beads
- ☐ Four 10mm faceted Czech fire-polished beads
- ☐ Two 8mm black onyx rondelles
- ☐ Four 6mm striped silver rounds

Water Fairy

The tranquil blues and greens of the ocean often mix to form a mystical quality. This necklace, which features a handmade glass fairy from Bickley Studios, is the perfect representation of this beautiful part of nature.

Tools

- ❑ Bead board
- ❑ Bead mat
- ❑ Crimping pliers
- ❑ Wire cutters

Materials

- ❑ 19-strand count original beading wire
- ❑ Two 2 x 2mm sterling silver crimp tubes
- ❑ 1 fairy pendant from Bickley Studios
- ❑ 1 marcasite box clasp
- ❑ Six 10mm black with blue flower lampwork rondelles
- ❑ Twelve 8mm light brown faceted Czech glass rondelles
- ❑ Twelve 12mm ocean blue teardrop-shaped dyed coral beads
- ❑ Twelve 18 x 10mm chrysocolla gemstone ovals

Memories of Margret

The blending together of different materials in this necklace is right on trend with today's styles and the use of mixed media. The ribbon closure gives the piece an especially feminine feel and allows the wearer to easily adjust its length.

Tools

❑ Bead board

❑ Bead mat

❑ Crimping pliers

❑ Wire cutters

Materials

❑ Antique brass chain

❑ Striped maroon ribbon

❑ 1 decoupage paper flower pendant

❑ 18 antique brass eye pins

❑ Two 20 x 15mm antique brass metal links

❑ Six 10 x 8mm vintage oval Czech glass beads

❑ Six 14mm faceted round zoisite gemstone beads

❑ Six 6mm faceted caramel and vanilla colored Czech glass beads

Boundless Inspiration

Theses beads were originally set together as part of a jewelry-making challenge.

Tools

- ❏ Bead board
- ❏ Bead mat
- ❏ Crimping pliers
- ❏ Wire cutters

Materials

- ❏ 19-strand count copper beading wire
- ❏ Six 2 x 2mm copper crimp tubes
- ❏ 1 copper toggle clasp
- ❏ Ten 8mm wooden rondelle beads
- ❏ Six 14mm coin-shaped beads
- ❏ Six 12mm green porcelain rondelle beads
- ❏ Eight 6mm green porcelain round beads
- ❏ Six 11mm round Rudraksha beads
- ❏ 2 etched copper metal rings
- ❏ Two 12 x 7mm copper filigree tubes
- ❏ Copper chain

Sets

Make your jewelry even more special by creating matching sets of necklaces and bracelets, necklaces and earrings, and more. Get creative and make sets that aren't exactly the same, but that share the same colors or basic designs. Have fun mixing and matching based on color, bead type, and decorative elements. It's amazing what you can do!

Swirling Pebbles Necklace and Bracelet

Dyed howlite beads bring a mix of bold colors to accent the necklace's center focal bead by Sher Berman of Sher Berman Glass Beads. The pewter beads have a similar swirl to tie everything together. Swirling Pebbles is a necklace meant to be noticeable.

Tools

- ❑ Bead board
- ❑ Bead mat
- ❑ Crimping pliers
- ❑ Wire cutters

Materials

- ❑ 19-strand count original beading wire
- ❑ Four 2 x 2mm sterling silver crimp tubes
- ❑ Glass focal pendent by Sher Berman of Sher Berman Glass Beads
- ❑ Dyed howlite nuggets in various colors and sizes.
- ❑ Six 12mm Pewter beads with swirls
- ❑ Eight 6mm round silver pewter beads
- ❑ 2 silver toggle clasps
- ❑ 1 dyed purple agate slice

Copper Pearls and Earrings

Copper accents, when mixed with Swarovski pearls, give an updated vintage appearance to this necklace and earrings set. The necklace has several components that are connected together to make one long piece. It can be worn as a single-, double-, or triple-strand piece. The earrings come together quickly and are tailor-made to complement the necklace.

Tools

- ❏ Bead board
- ❏ Bead mat
- ❏ Crimping pliers
- ❏ Wire cutters

Materials

- ❏ 19-strand count copper beading wire
- ❏ Fourteen 2 x 2mm copper crimp tubes
- ❏ 1 square copper metal clasp
- ❏ 1 pair of copper post earring findings
- ❏ Two 2" (51mm) copper eye pins
- ❏ Six 18mm copper metal filigree round beads
- ❏ Six 18mm copper metal single layer daisies with rhinestones
- ❏ One 18mm copper metal double layer daisy with rhinestones
- ❏ One 18mm copper metal rose with rhinestones
- ❏ One 23mm copper metal filigree diamond-shaped link with rhinestones
- ❏ Eleven 8mm copper rings
- ❏ Eleven 6mm crystal Swarovski crystal faceted rounds
- ❏ Forty-nine 10mm Bordeaux Swarovski crystal pearls
- ❏ Fourteen 10mm cream Swarovski crystal pearls
- ❏ Eighteen 10mm antique brass Swarovski crystal pearls

Surfing Convertible

This piece is hiding a secret: You can wear the necklace as shown, or detach the beaded section from the leather and wear it as a functional bracelet. Either way, this convertible necklace/bracelet combination will make a splash.

Tools

- ❏ Bead board
- ❏ Bead mat
- ❏ Flat-nose pliers
- ❏ Crimping pliers
- ❏ Wire cutters

Materials

- ❏ 19-strand count original beading wire
- ❏ Dark brown leather cord
- ❏ 4 silver folded crimps
- ❏ Two 2 x 2mm sterling silver crimp tubes
- ❏ 3 lobster claw and jump ring clasps
- ❏ 34 ocean blue heishi beads
- ❏ Five 12mm shell beads
- ❏ Ten 6mm silver bumpy lantern-shaped spacer beads

Inspirational Ideas

Here are some finished projects to help spark and inspire your creativity. Use them as templates or starting points for future beading projects. With the countless materials available, there is no limit to the number or variety of pieces you can create!

Southwestern Lace.

Autumn Beginnings

SIMPLE BEGINNINGS: Beading

Black and White Elegance

Elphaba's Necklace

SIMPLE BEGINNINGS: Beading

Hot! Hot! Hot!

Mother's Day Necklace

On the Rocks

Reflections of Lorelei

Summer Blooms

Most craft and variety stores carry an excellent assortment of supplies. If you need something special, ask your local store to contact the following companies:

Bead on Beads, Texas
www.beadonbeads.com
972-241-5868

The Bead Smith by Helby Import Co.
www.helby.com
723-969-5300

Beadalon, Pennsylvania
www.Beadalon.com
866-423-2325

Beadphoria Boutique, Illinois
www.BeadphoriaBoutique.com
224-305-3321

Blue Moon Beads by Creativity Inc., California
www.BlueMoonBeads.com
800-727-2727

Cousins Corporation of America, Florida
www.cousin.com
800-366-2687

Dakota Stones, Minnesota
www.DakotaStones.com
866-871-1990

Darice, Ohio
www.Darice.com
800-321-1494

Euro Tool, Missouri
www.eurotool.com
800-552-3131

Halcraft USA
www.Halcraft.com
914-840-0505
Products sold in retail stores nationwide.

John Bead Corporation
www.johnbead.com
888-755-9055
Products sold in retail stores nationwide.

Plaid Enterprises
www.plaidonline.com
800-842-4197
Products sold in retail stores nationwide.

Ranger, New Jersey
www.RangerInk.com
732-389-3535
Products sold in retail stores nationwide.

Rings and Things, Washington
www.rings-things.com
800-366-2156

Rio Grande, New Mexico
www.riogrande.com
800-545-6566

Simply Swank, Washington
www.simplyswank.net
800-810-4350

Soft Flex Company
www.softflexcompany.com
866-925-3539
Products sold in retail stores nationwide.

Super Time International, Maryland
www.supertimebeads.com
800-878-2943

Swarovski Elements, Lichtenstein
www.create-your-style.com
800-388-8842

Vintaj Natural Brass Company, Illinois
www.vintaj.com
866-228-1846

Artisan On-Line Marketplaces

ArtFire
www.artfire.com

Big Cartel
www.bigcartel.com

Etsy
www.etsy.com

Groove Press
www.groovepress.com

Bead Artisans

Acme Bead Company
www.acmebeadcompany.com
920-55-7446

Bickley Studios
www.BickleyStudios.com

Cindy Gimbrone Beads
www.cindygimbronebeads.com

Heather and Pamela Wynn
www.etsy.com/shop/swoondimples

Earthenwood Studio
www.earthenwoodstudio.com
248-548-4793

Gelly Davis
www.GellyButton.com

Green Girl Studios, North Carolina
www.greengirlstudios.com
828-298-2263

Holly's Folly Glass Beads
www.hollysfolly.com

Jennifer Jangles
www.Jangles.net
706-207-9032

Joan Miller Porcelain Beads
www.JoanMiller.com

Lori Anderson
www.lorianderson.net

Lucid Moon Studios
www.etsy.com/shop/lucidmoonsupplies

Maybeads
www.maybeads.etsy.com

Nikki Thornburg
www.thornburgbeadstudio.com

Mallory Hoffman
www.rosebud101.com

Sher Berman Glass Beads
412 Castlewood Ln.
Deerfield, Illinois 60015
847-405-9981

Index

Acquisition editor: **Peg Couch**

Copy editors: **Paul Hambke and Heather Stauffer**

Cover and page designer: **Lindsay Hess**

Layout designer: **Ashley Millhouse**

Editor: **Katie Weeber**

Proofreader: **Lynda Jo Runkle**

More Great Books from Design Originals

Essential Links for Wire Jewelry

The Ultimate Reference Guide to Creating More Than 300 Intermediate-Level Wire Jewelry Links

By Lora S. Irish

Discover over 300 links you can add to your wire jewelry. You'll return to this guide again and again for inspiration.

ISBN: 978-1-57421-345-4
$9.99 • 32 Pages

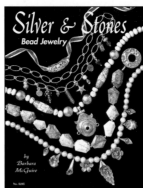

Silver & Stones Bead Jewelry

By Barbara McGuire

Play with natural wonders sculpted with age old craftsmanship and pride and design unique pieces.

ISBN: 978-1-57421-605-9

$12.99 • 36 Pages

Bead Happy

Simple Jewelry for Everyday Wear!
By Suzanne McNeill

Experiment with silver and gold, glass, crystals and natural materials such as turquoise, howlite, red coral and pearls.

ISBN: 978-1-57421-296-9
$8.99 • 20 Pages

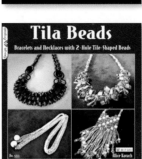

Tila Beads

Bracelets and Necklaces with 2 Hole Tile Shaped Beads
By Alice Korach

Use these exciting new beads from Miyuki to discover new possibilities. Fabulous bracelets, necklaces and keychains using TILA Beads.

ISBN: 978-1-57421-402-4
$16.99 • 52 Pages

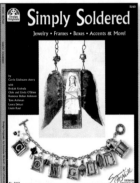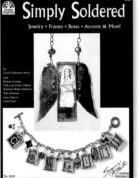

Simply Soldered

Jewelry Frames Boxes Accents & More
By Carrie Edelmann-Avery

Make mixed media art from personal keepsakes that will last long enough to pass down for several generations.

ISBN: 978-1-57421-553-3
$12.99 • 36 Pages

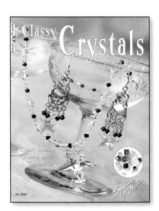

Classy Crystals

Simple And Stylish. Create Dazzling Jewelry With Crystals
By Suzanne McNeill

Create a glittering necklace, bracelet or earrings to suit your every mood without breaking the budget! Beads, wire & crystals and a few tools are all it takes.

ISBN: 978-1-57421-295-2
$8.99 • 20 Pages

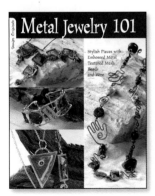

Metal Jewelry 101

Stylized Pieces with Embossed Metal, Textured Mesh Beads, and Wire
By Linda Peterson

Creating fashionable metal and wire jewelry is easy, enjoyable and requires only inexpensive tools.

ISBN: 978-1-57421-275-4
$8.99 • 20 Pages

Beads & Trinkets

Embellishing With Idea-Ology™ Findings, Doodads, Grungeboard™ And Trinkets
By Lisa Stephens

Using trinkets and beads, it is easy to transform your life experiences into stunning, wearable jewelry that express a style that is all your own.

ISBN: 978-1-57421-325-6
$8.99 • 20 Pages

Look for These Books at Your Local Bookstore or Specialty Retailer

To order direct, call **800-457-9112** or visit *www.FoxChapelPublishing.com*
By mail, please send check or money order + S&H to:
Fox Chapel Publishing, 1970 Broad Street, East Petersburg, PA 17520

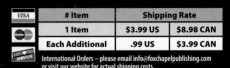

# Item	Shipping Rate	
1 Item	$3.99 US	$8.98 CAN
Each Additional	.99 US	$3.99 CAN

International Orders – please email info@foxchapelpublishing.com or visit our website for actual shipping costs.